DEHYDRATION OF FRUITS

(A PROGRESS REPORT)

BY

W. V. CRUESS AND A. W. CHRISTIE

British Library Cataloguing-in-Publication Data
A catalogue record for this book is available from the
British Library

Preserving and Canning Food: Jams, Jellies and Pickles

Food preservation has permeated every culture, at nearly every moment in history. To survive in an often hostile and confusing world, ancient man was forced to harness nature. In cold climates he froze foods on the ice, and in tropical areas, he dried them in the sun. Today, methods of preserving food commonly involve preventing the growth of bacteria, fungi (such as yeasts), and other micro-organisms, as well as retarding the oxidation of fats that cause rancidity. Many processes designed to conserve food will involve a number of different food preservation methods. Preserving fruit by turning it into jam, for example, involves boiling (to reduce the fruit's moisture content and to kill bacteria, yeasts, etc.), sugaring (to prevent their re-growth) and sealing within an airtight jar (to prevent recontamination). Preservation with the use of either honey or sugar was well known to the earliest cultures, and in ancient Greece, fruits kept in honey were common fare. Quince, mixed with honey, semi-dried and then packed tightly into jars was a particular speciality. This method was taken, and improved upon by the Romans, who *cooked* the quince and honey - producing a solidified texture which kept for much longer. These techniques have remained popular into the modern age, and especially during the high-tide of imperialism, when trading between Europe, India and the Orient was at its peak. This fervour for trade had two fold consequences; the need to preserve a variety of foods - hence we see more 'pickling', and the arrival of sugar cane in Europe. Preserving fruits, i.e. making jams and jellies became especially popular in Northern European countries, as without enough natural sunlight to dry food, this was a fail safe method to increase longevity. Jellies were actually most commonly used for savoury items; some foods, such as eels, naturally form a protein gel when cooked - and this dish became especially popular in the East End of London, where they were (and are) eaten with mashed potatoes. Pickling; the technique of preserving foods in vinegar (or other anti-microbial substances such as brine, alcohol or vegetable oil) also has a long history, again gaining precedence with the Romans, who made a concentrated fish pickle sauce called 'garum'. 'Ketchup' was originally an oriental fish brine which travelled the spice route to Europe (some time during the sixteenth century), and eventually to America, where sugar was finally added to it. The increase in trade with the sub-continent also meant that spices became a common-place item in European kitchens, and they were widely used in pickles to create new and exciting recipes. Soon chutneys, relishes, piccalillis, mustards, and ketchups were routine condiments. Amusingly, Worcester sauce was discovered from a forgotten barrel of special relish in the basement of the Lea and Perrins Chemist shop! As is evident, the story of food preservation, and specifically the modern usages of jams, jellies and pickles encompasses far more than just culinary history. Ancient civilisations, nineteenth century colonialism and accidental discoveries all played a part in creating this staple of our modern diet.

DAVID P. BARROWS, President of the University.

EXPERIMENT STATION STAFF

HEADS OF DIVISIONS

THOMAS FORSYTH HUNT, Dean.
EDWARD J. WICKSON, Horticulture (Emeritus).
————— —————, Director of Resident Instruction.
CLARENCE M. HARING, Veterinary Science, Director Agricultural Experiment Station.
B. H. CROCHERON, Director of Agricultural Extension.
JAMES T. BARRETT, Acting Director of Citrus Experiment Station, Plant Pathology.
WILLIAM A. SETCHELL, Botany.
MYER E. JAFFA, Nutrition.
RALPH E. SMITH, Plant Pathology.
JOHN W. GILMORE, Agronomy.
CHARLES F. SHAW, Soil Technology.
JOHN W. GREGG, Landscape Gardening and Floriculture.
FREDERIC T. BIOLETTI, Viticulture and Fruit Products.
WARREN T. CLARKE, Agricultural Extension.
ERNEST B. BABCOCK, Genetics.
GORDON H. TRUE, Animal Husbandry.
WALTER MULFORD, Forestry.
FRITZ W. WOLL, Animal Nutrition.
W. P. KELLEY, Agricultural Chemistry.
H. J. QUAYLE, Entomology.
ELWOOD MEAD, Rural Institutions.
H. S. REED, Plant Physiology.
J. C. WHITTEN, Pomology.
*FRANK ADAMS, Irrigation Investigations.
C. L. ROADHOUSE, Dairy Industry.
R. L. ADAMS, Farm Management.
F. L. GRIFFIN, Agricultural Education.
JOHN E. DOUGHERTY, Poultry Husbandry.
W. B. HERMS, Entomology and Parasitology.
D. R. HOAGLAND, Plant Nutrition.
L. J. FLETCHER, Agricultural Engineering.
EDWIN C. VOORHIES, Assistant to the Dean.

DIVISION OF VITICULTURE AND FRUIT PRODUCTS

F. T. BIOLETTI	G. BAROVETTO
W. V. CRUESS	A. J. WINKLER
A. W. CHRISTIE	J. H. IRISH
L. O. BONNET	

---

* In coöperation with office of Public Roads and Rural Engineering, U. S. Department of Agriculture.

DEHYDRATION OF FRUITS
(A PROGRESS REPORT)

By W. V. CRUESS and A. W. CHRISTIE.

CONTENTS

The production of dried fruits in California has increased rapidly during the past decade. The total rose from approximately 185,000 tons in 1910 to approximately 360,000 tons in 1920. The orchard and vineyard acreage has, moreover, increased notably during the past five years. In 1919 and 1920, about 275,000 acres were planted. During the 1920 planting season, nurseries were unable to supply the demand for trees and vines. An increased output of fruit is therefore to be expected within the next three to five years, as the newly planted orchards and vineyards come into bearing.

It is doubtful whether the fresh fruit markets and canneries will absorb all of this increase and even under the most favorable market conditions, it is probable that a greater proportion than at present, of certain fruit crops must be preserved and marketed in the dried form. It will therefore be necessary to increase our markets for dried fruits and other fruit products if fruit growing is to continue to be profitable. This can be aided by improving the quality of these products, particularly of the dried fruits, and by diversifying them. Dehydration offers a means of producing dried fruits of new forms and, in some instances, of better quality.

The sale of one important fruit product directly affects the marketing of other fruit products and of fresh fruit. If the quality of dried fruit is high, it is naturally more in demand and commands a higher price than an inferior product. However, much fruit that is unsuitable for marketing, either fresh or for canning, can be made into an acceptable dehydrated product which can be profitably marketed. The utilization of such fruit for dehydration prevents waste and aids in stablizing the market for all fruit products.

In California all fruits except apples are usually dried in the sun. Twenty-five to thirty years ago, in the early days of the state's fruit industry, most fruit was dried by artificial heat. It has been stated that wire screen trays were used for the first fruit dried in the sun in order that the product should bear the imprint of the screen in imitation of the artificially dried product. Some sun-dried fruit, however, was marketed on its own merits, and being superior to the average artificially dried fruit, it soon came into greater favor. In time, in California, sun-dried prunes and raisins displaced the product of the artificial driers.

Methods of dehydration have been improved recently and it is now contended by operators of modern dehydraters that properly dehydrated fruits are equal or even superior to the sun-dried fruits, and that dehydration possesses certain advantages over sun-drying.

The advantages claimed are:

1. That dehydrated fruits, when cooked, more nearly resemble the fresh fruit in color and flavor.

2. That dehydrated fruits are produced under more sanitary conditions.

3. That dehydration permits more exact control of quality and yield.

4. That less land and fewer trays are required to dehydrate a given tonnage of fruit.

5. That dehydration makes it possible to combine all the steps of drying and packing in one building.

In seasons of early rains the utility of dehydraters in preventing loss of fruit and in reclaiming rain-damaged prunes and grapes has been fully demonstrated. It has also been conclusively proved that dehydraters have a place in fruit-growing sections in which there is even in normal years insufficient sunshine to permit successful sun-drying.

It must not be forgotten, however, that California has established a reputation for the excellent quality of her sun-dried fruits and that the great bulk of our dried fruits will probably continue to be sun-dried, however successful dehydration may become. At great expense to the fruit-growing associations, a widespread demand for ''Sunsweet'' prunes and apricots, ''Blue Ribbon'' sun-dried peaches and ''Sun-Maid'' raisins has been created. It is believed that dehydrated fruits of high quality will find new markets not necessarily in direct competition with the sun-dried fruits and to that extent provide an increased outlet for the crops of our rapidly extending orchards.

With this viewpoint in mind and also to test the validity of the claims of superiority made for dehydration, investigations extending over the past three years have been conducted by members of the Fruit Products Laboratory. Though the investigations are not yet complete, the widespread interest in the subject makes it advisable to publish certain important results.

This publication gives the results of investigations and observations on the dehydration of the more important varieties of fruits in California. Pears, peaches, apricots, and grapes were dehydrated experimentally in commercial quantities at the University Farm. Other fruits were dried there in lots of five to five hundred pounds and also in the laboratory dehydraters at Berkeley. Observations and experiments were also made in a number of commercial plants.

DEFINITIONS

Dehydration is at present defined industrially as the drying of foods by artificially produced heat under carefully controlled conditions of temperature, humidity, and air flow. The object of this process may be accomplished by many devices, provided they conform to certain principles governing the proper drying of fruit. The writers published in 1920 in Bulletin 322 their views upon the terminology of dried fruits. At that time, it was stated that the term "dried" should apply to all dried fruits, whether sun-dried or dried by artificial heat, and that "evaporated" and "dehydrated" should be of equal value in designating fruits dried by artificial heat. We see no reason at present for modifying these recommendations. The fruit-drying industry itself, however, has definitely favored the word "dehydrated" to designate artificially dried food products of superior quality in preference to the word "evaporated." It therefore appears that commercial usage may cause the adoption of the former term in the dried fruit trade.

The terms drier, dehydrater, and evaporator are now used more or less indiscriminately. The word drier is usually considered to be a general term applicable to any apparatus used to remove moisture from fruit or other materials. A dehydrater is usually understood to be more efficient and to permit of more careful regulation than an evaporator.

In order to avoid confusion, the following definitions are used in this bulletin. The writers do not consider these definitions final nor necessarily authoritative.

1. *Drier:* A general term, applicable to all machines used for drying fruits or other materials. Examples: hop drier, cement drier, varnish drier, lumber drier, etc.

2. *Evaporator:* A drying machine without forced draft and which does not permit of accurate control of temperature, humidity, or air velocity.

3. *Dehydrater:* A drying machine with forced draft and in which the temperature, relative humidity, and air velocity can be accurately controlled.

PREPARATION

The effect of various methods of preparing fruits for dehydration on the rate of drying and on the quality of the finished product was studied both at the University Farm and in the laboratory at Berkeley.

Ripening of Bartlett Pears: Approximately 3500 pounds of windfall and cull Bartlett pears from a single orchard were divided into three portions. One lot was placed in lug boxes and another on screen trays. Both lots were allowed to ripen under an open shed. The third lot was stratified between layers of straw in the sun. The fruit in each lot was sorted several times during ripening.

The ripened pears were sorted for removal of spoiled fruit and were then trimmed and halved for drying. The total loss from sorting and trimming for the lot ripened on screen trays was 7.4 per cent; for that in lug boxes 8.6 per cent, and for the lot in straw 8.5 per cent.

The fruit on screen trays ripened less uniformly than that in lug boxes or straw and required a larger number of sortings during ripening. These disadvantages counterbalance the advantage of slightly smaller loss from rot in this method of ripening.

Effect of Maturity on Yield and Quality: Orchard run Muir peaches were sorted into three lots of approximately 150 pounds each. One lot represented hard green, the second lot, hard ripe, and the third, soft ripe fruit. The peaches were cut, pitted, spread on $2' \times 3'$ field trays, and sulfured for five hours. They were dried in the sun for three days and then in the stack for five. Table I gives the yields of dried products and their composition.

TABLE I

Effect of Maturity on Yield and Composition of Dried Peaches

Degree of ripeness	Per cent of pits	Drying ratio	Water per cent in dry product	Lbs. dry fruit per 100 lbs. fresh		Sugar per cent in dried fruit	
				As weighed	On 25 per cent water basis	As weighed	On 25 per cent moisture basis
Soft ripe	6.5	4.86:1	18.1	20.6	22.5	48.5	43.9
Hard ripe	5.9	4.64:1	19.4	21.6	23.2	48.5	45.1
Hard green	4.3	5.11:1	18.1	19.6	21.5	45.0	41.2

On a uniform moisture basis of 25 per cent the yield from green fruit was appreciably less than that from ripe fruit. Likewise, the sugar content of the former was considerably less than that of the latter. The dried green fruit was astringent and sour in flavor and of an unattractive greyish brown color. The dried hard-ripe fruit was lighter in color and of less pleasing flavor and texture than the dried soft-ripe fruit. The quality of dried pears and apricots was affected similarly by maturity.

Muscat and Sultanina (Thompson seedless) grapes of 20° Balling yielded very inferior products of reddish color and sour flavor.

Grapes of the same varieties at 25° Balling yielded raisins of excellent flavor and appearance by similar treatment.

As a result of these experiments and of practical experience, it is recommended that all fruits used for dehydration be thoroughly ripe.

Comparison of Lye Dipping and Blanching: Prunes are usually lye dipped before dehydration, although in some plants the fruit is dried without preliminary treatment and in others the prunes are blanched in steam before drying. In order to compare the rate of drying of untreated, of steamed, and of lye-dipped prunes, an experiment was conducted in an air-blast laboratory dehydrater. One lot was dipped in boiling 1 per cent lye solution, another steamed on trays in a heavy jet of steam for five minutes, and a third was untreated. The untreated fruit required 30 per cent more time to dry than the dipped prunes. The steamed fruit dried slightly more rapidly than the dipped fruit.

The tests were repeated in a commercial evaporator in which the air velocity was very low. There was little difference in the rates of drying in this instance, although the untreated fruit dried less evenly than that which had been steamed or dipped.

In a large natural draft evaporator, dipped prunes lost 54 per cent of their weight in 31 hours at 140° to 145° F., and undipped prunes under the same conditions lost 51 per cent. This difference is small and of no practical significance.

In a commercial dehydrater in which the velocity of the air across the trays was high (about 600 feet per minute) dipped prunes dried in approximately one-half the time required for untreated fruit.

From these experiments, it seems evident that lye dipping does not appreciably hasten drying when the air velocity is low, but does so materially when the air velocity is high. Undipped prunes dry practically as rapidly as dipped prunes in evaporators of low air velocity because the limiting factor in such instances is probably not the ability of the fruit to give up its water rapidly, but rather the limited capacity of the low air flow to supply sufficient heat for rapid evaporation of the moisture.

Dehydrated steamed prunes were redder in color and more translucent than dehydrated lye-dipped prunes. Prolonged steaming caused bursting of the fruit and sticking to the trays. With ample steam supply, two to five minutes' exposure to steam was found sufficient, but in instances where the steam supply was inadequate, a longer period of treatment was required. The fruit should be heated through completely, but heating should not be continued long enough to unduly soften it.

Certain varieties of grapes, such as Tokays and Emperors, responded satisfactorily to steaming. Wine grapes, such as Zinfandel and Alicante Bouschet varieties, softened badly when steamed and lost a great deal of their juice. For a dehydrater in which all common varieties of grapes are to be dried, lye dipping is more satisfactory than steaming. Plants in which only Tokay grapes are dried can use steaming to advantage.

Dipping for 5 to 20 seconds in a boiling 2 per cent sodium carbonate solution, followed by rinsing in water, checked the skins of Royal Anne and Black Tartarian cherries more satisfactorily than did dilute lye solutions. The lye tended to peel the more tender fruit, although good results were obtained commercially by dipping cull cherries for 10 to 30 seconds in a boiling solution containing 1 per cent of Canner's alkali, a mixture of lye and carbonate. Dipping reduced the drying time approximately one half and was found to be more satisfactory than blanching in steam or hot water.

Pitting: All peaches and apricots dehydrated at the University Farm in 1920 were pitted by hand before drying. Royal apricots yielded 7.7 per cent of fresh pits and 5.9 per cent of sun-dried pits upon the basis of the fresh uncut fruit.

Muir peaches yielded 6.1 per cent of fresh pits and 5.3 per cent of sun-dried pits.

Small quantities of Royal Anne and Black Tartarian cherries were pitted with a hand power pitter, causing a loss in each instance of 18 per cent of the fresh weight.

Peeling: Halved Muir peaches were peeled by immersion for 30 seconds in boiling 5 per cent lye solution and rinsing in cold water to remove adhering lye and softened skins. . The loss in lye peeling was 4.5 per cent of the weight of the pitted fruit. The lye-peeled fruit required less sulfuring, dried more rapidly, and yielded a more attractive finished product than did the unpeeled fruit. Exposure to sulfur fumes for one hour was sufficient. The lye-peeled fruit darkened rapidly unless placed in the sulfur fumes very soon after peeling. Dipping in dilute salt solution after peeling, reduced the tendency to darken. Lye peeled peaches gave trouble by sticking to wooden trays. This difficulty can be overcome by covering the to wooden trays. The application of "slab" oil to the trays did not prevent sticking.

Whole ripe Bartlett pears required an immersion of 20 seconds in boiling 10 per cent lye solution and firm ripe pears 30 to 40 seconds. Green fruit did not respond satisfactorily to lye peeling. After dipping in the boiling lye solution, the skins were removed by agitation of the fruit in a wire-screen basket in cold water. The peeled fruit was then halved and cored. The loss by lye peeling was 20 per cent; by lye peeling and coring, 34 per cent, and by hand peeling and coring 36 per cent. It was found necessary to immerse the lye-peeled fruit in dilute brine (3 to 5 per cent salt) or to wet the fruit on the trays with this solution, in order to prevent darkening before it was placed in the sulfur house. Peeled pears required only one hour of sulfuring as compared with 24 hours for the unpeeled fruit. The peeled and cored pears yielded a very attractive dehydrated product which, after cooking, closely resembled canned pears.

A narrow strip of peel cut around the pear from stem to calyx, followed by halving and coring, prevented the edges of the fruit from curling during drying. This product was much superior in appearance to fruit that was merely halved without removal of stem, core, or the narrow strip of peel.

Slicing: All fruits dry more rapidly when cut in thin pieces. Less sulfuring is required and the finished product cooks more rapidly than the whole or halved fruit. Sliced dehydrated pears, apricots, persimmons, and peaches were very attractive in appearance and decidedly "different" from the usual sun-dried fruits. Thinly sliced or cubed dehydrated apples were superior for culinary purposes to the usual ring style.

Sliced Bartlett pears were dehydrated in less than 6 hours, lye-peeled halves in 16 to 18 hours, and unpeeled halves in 36 to 48 hours under similar drying conditions. The sliced product was excellent when used for sauces or pies.

As a result of these experiments, the writers wish to call attention to the excellence of apricots, peaches, pears, and apples that have been thinly sliced, cubed, or shredded before dehydration.

Tray Capacity: The amount of fruit that may be placed upon each square foot of tray surface varies greatly with the variety and size of the fruit, its method of preparation, and the system of dehydration employed.

At the University Farm, the dehydrater trays held two pounds of medium-size halved apricots per square foot; three pounds of medium-size halved Muir peaches, three pounds of halved pears, two and one-half to three and one-half pounds of prunes one layer deep, and three to four pounds of grapes. Thinly sliced fruit tends to form masses on the tray which impede air flow and thereby retard drying. Consequently, trays should be loaded less heavily with such fruit than with large pieces.

In dehydraters using high air velocity (500–1000 feet per minute) and high initial temperatures (190° F., or above) the trays can be much more heavily loaded than where lower air velocities and lower temperatures (110° to 170° F.) are used. For example, trays of dipped cherries containing two and four pounds per square foot respectively, dried equally rapidly in a laboratory dehydrator, using an initial temperature of 210° F., a finishing temperature of 170° F., and an air velocity of 1000 feet per minute. Similar results were obtained with sliced apples.

At the temperatures and air velocities at present employed in commercial dehydration, the rate of drying is very materially affected by the load per square foot of tray surface. The loads per square foot of tray surface recommended for various fruits to be dehydrated by the counter current system are given in Table VIII.

Sulfuring: The natural color of most fruits is retained by exposure of the prepared fruit to the fumes of burning sulfur before drying. The time of sulfuring necessary varies with the variety of fruit and its previous treatment. For example, thinly sliced Bartlett pears require 20 to 30 minutes sulfuring, lye-peeled pears 1 to 3 hours, and unpeeled halved pears 24 to 36 hours. Sliced apricots require 30 minutes sulfuring as compared to one hour for the halved fruit. Immersion of the cut fruit in dilute brine reduces the time of sulfuring required, especially for white fruits, such as pears and apples.

As a result of the investigations of the past two seasons, the periods of sulfuring given in Table VIII are recommended for the various fruits.

Galvanized screen trays have proved unsatisfactory for the drying of fruits that require sulfuring. The sulfurous acid formed by solution of sulfur dioxide (sulfur fumes) in the fruit juices rapidly dissolves the zinc coating, imparting a metallic flavor to the fruit and exposing the iron wire of the screen. Iron causes blackening of white fruits by the reaction of iron salts with the fruit tannins. Screen trays are shortlived when used for sulfured fruits, and must be replaced frequently. Attempts have been made to coat the trays with paraffin, slab oil, varnish, can lacquer, various paints, and other protective coatings, but, to date, no satisfactory material has been found. Wooden slat trays have given excellent service in the University Farm and other dehydraters. They are not corroded and are less expensive than screen trays.

There is a growing demand for unsulfured dried fruit. Untreated, sun-dried, or dehydrated cut fruits, such as apples, peaches, etc., are of an unattractive brown color. Sliced fruits retain much of their original color without excessive browning if immersed in cold dilute (3 to 5 per cent) salt solution for several minutes immediately after cutting. Unpeeled halved fruit retains its fresh color on the cut surface but darkens beneath the skin. Blanching on the trays in steam gives fairly satisfactory results with white grapes, Tokay grapes, and with peeled halved pears and peaches, but fails to produce an attractive color in unpeeled halved pears, peaches, and apricots. Steaming softens berries and apples so much that the dried product is of very unattractive appearance. Berries, cherries, prunes, and persimmons retain their color very well without sulfuring before drying.

YIELDS OF DEHYDRATED FRUITS

Yields of dehydrated grapes, peaches, pears, and apricots were determined at the University Farm on lots of five to thirty-five tons of fresh fruit. Yields for a number of other fruits were determined in the laboratory. These data are given in Table II.

The yields vary according to the locality in which the fruit is grown, the season, the maturity of the fruit, and the variety. For example, the average drying ratio for all grape varieties dried at the University Farm in 1919 was approximately 3 :1, and in 1920, it was 3.64 :1. It must be expected, therefore, that considerable variation from the yields given in Table II will be found in practice. The data are useful, however, in indicating the approximate comparative yields of various fruits and the loss in preparation.

TEMPERATURE

The temperature of the air used in dehydration not only greatly affects the time required for drying, but also the quality of the finished product. In order to secure large capacity and minimum operating costs, it is necessary to use the highest temperature that will not materially injure the product. Practically all dehydraters which involve a progressive movement of the fruit through the drying chamber have used the "counter current system," which means that the fruit is introduced into relatively cold moist air (100° F. to 130° F.) and moved toward a region of warmer, drier air until the drying is completed at temperatures of 150° F. to 180° F. Recent tests on a commercial scale indicate that this system, at least for certain fruits, is not so efficient as the "parallel current system" discussed in another report of this Station. The "critical temperature" for any fruit is the temperature at which, when the fruit is almost dry, it may undergo undesirable changes in color or flavor. In the "counter

TABLE II

SHRINKAGE IN THE PREPARATION AND DEHYDRATION OF VARIOUS FRUITS

Fruit	Per cent of fresh fruit unsorted					Drying ratio	
	Sorted uncut fruit	Prepared fruit cut, pitted, dipped or hulled	Prepared and peeled fruit	Loss in preparation	Dried fruit	Gross fresh to net dry	Prepared fresh to net dry
Royal Apricots from Winters	100	92.3	....	7.7	17.2	5.8:1	5.4:1
Muir peaches from Winters, unpeeled	96.4	90.3	....	9.7	20.9	4.8:1 .	4.3:1
Muir peaches from Winters, lye peeled	96.4	90.3	86.2	13.8	19.9	5.0:1	4.3:1
Bartlett pears from Sacramento, unpeeled	97.9	91.7	....	8.3	19.5	5.1:1	4.7:1
Bartlett pears from Sacramento, lye peeled and cored	97.9	91.7	60.5	39.5	12.9	7.8:1	4.7:1
Grapes, all varieties, stemmed, Univ.Farm, 1920	100	100	100	0	27.5	3.6:1	....
Newtown apples from Watsonville	100	....	75	25	12.3	8.3:1	6.1:1
Loganberries from Sebastopol	100	100	100	0	21.1	4.7:1	4.7:1
Cherries, Black Tartarian from San Leandro, not pitted	100	100	100	0	33.5	3.0:1	3.0:1
Cherries, Black Tartarian, from San Leandro, pitted and stemmed	100	80	....	20	23.7	4.2:1	3.4:1
Cherries, Royal Anne, from Napa, not pitted	100	....	....	....	27.7	3.6:1	....
Cherries, Royal Anne, from Napa, pitted and stemmed	100	80	....	20	23.5	4.3:1	3.4:1
Raspberries from Oakland	100	100	100	0	14.8	6.8:1	6.8:1
Strawberries, four varieties, from Salinas	100	96.4	....	3.6	16.7	5.9:1	....

current system," this temperature is the maximum which can be used, while in the "parallel current system," this temperature must not be exceeded in the final stages of drying, although much higher temperatures can be used while the fruit still contains an excess of moisture.

The maximum advisable finishing temperatures for each of the more important fruits are given in Table VIII. These temperatures were obtained during the operation of the University Farm and other dehydraters operated on the "counter current system." It is likely that these temperatures may be seriously modified during the 1921 season by the use of the "parallel current system." In the latter method, the critical or finishing temperature is accompanied by a relatively high humidity which partially protects the fruit from injury, whereas in the "counter current system" the air at the finishing temperature is generally rather dry, a condition more conducive to injury.

Experiments by Gadgil, Winkler, and Bjarnason, graduate students in the Fruit Products laboratory, indicated rapid loss of sugar when raisins were heated to 185° F. after becoming nearly dry. At lower temperatures, the effects were negligible unless the raisins were allowed to become very much over-dried, a condition which should never occur in a commercial plant. The extent of such sugar loss is indicated in Table III. Another test in a commercial plant showed that Alicante Bouschet grapes dried at 190° F. to 200° F., to 10 per cent moisture, for stemming, contained 5 per cent less sugar than grapes from the same lot dried to the same moisture content at 165° F.

Apricots have been finished at 175° F., but this temperature is apt to cause injury. For best results, 165° F. should not be exceeded. Peaches are a little more sensitive to injury than apricots, especially in the pit cavity and on the hairy skin. For this fruit, 160° F. is considered the highest temperature advisable during the last stages of dehydration. Pears finished above 145° F. become yellowish brown when nearly dry. Therefore, if a white product is desired, 145° F. should not be exceeded. If a translucent product similar to the highly sulfured sun-dried pear is desired, drying should be conducted at 110° F. to 120° F., although such an operation would probably not be economical. Prunes can not be safely finished above 170° F., although temperatures as high as 190° F. have been successfully used where the prunes dried very evenly and were removed from the dehydrater while still containing over 20 per cent moisture. The grapes dehydrated at the University Farm were finished at 165° F., which gave an exceptionally good product with natural color and flavor. Wine grapes dehydrated commercially at 185° F. had brown-colored flesh and a carmelized flavor. Sliced sulfured apples will withstand 160° F. when dry, without browning, while at 180° F. the product turns brown even before sufficiently dry. Fresh apples were not injured at 220° F., while still high in moisture. Both black and white cherries were successfully finished at 170° F., using either the parallel or counter current systems.

TABLE III

LOSS OF SUGAR FROM RAISINS SUBJECTED TO VARIOUS TEMPERATURES

Temperature	Hours exposed	Per cent of sugar loss
140° F.	8	0.6
140° F.	16	0.8
140° F.	32	1.0
167° F.	8	1.3
167° F.	16	1.9
167° F.	32	6.2
185° F.	8	8.7
185° F.	16	12.2
185° F.	32	14.9

RELATIVE HUMIDITY

The rate of evaporation from a free water surface in air at a given temperature varies inversely with the relative humidity of the air; that is, the higher the relative humidity, the less rapid the rate of evaporation. Relative humidity of air may be defined as its percentage of saturation with moisture vapor. Air completely saturated with water vapor at a given temperature is at 100 per cent relative humidity; air at the same temperature containing one-half the amount of water vapor that it is capable of absorbing is at 50 per cent relative humidity. The absolute amount of water vapor that air can absorb (within certain temperature limits) approximately doubles with each 27° F. rise in temperature. For example, air at 177° F. and 25 per cent relative humidity contains twice as much water vapor as air at 150° F. and 25 per cent relative humidity. In other words, the higher the temperature, the greater is the moisture carrying capacity of the air. Therefore, theoretically, high temperatures and low relative humidities should be employed in dehydration.

The evaporation of water from many fruits, however, does not follow closely the law of evaporation of water from a free surface. Large pieces of fruit, such as halved pears, peaches, or whole Imperial prunes, case-harden if the relative humidity is so low and the temperature so high that the moisture is removed more rapidly from the surface than it diffuses from the interior of the fruit. Case-hardening retards the rate of evaporation because it impedes the diffusion of water to the surface of the fruit.

In experiments on pears and peaches, it was found that case-hardening was materially reduced by increasing the relative humidity of the air at 150° F. to 30 to 35 per cent. A humidity of 20 to 25 per cent was obtained by recirculation of the exhaust air and the remaining 10 to 15 per cent was gained by the introduction of fine sprays of water into the heating chamber.

Thinly sliced fruits (e.g. pears, apricots, and peaches), dipped grapes, small to medium size prunes, and dipped cherries do not case-harden seriously. Therefore, air of high initial temperature (190° to 210° F.) and low relative humidity can be employed successfully with such fruits. The minimum relative humidities of air at the finishing temperature found satisfactory for the various fruits are given in Table VIII, Column 5.

DRYING TIME

The time required for the dehydration of a given fruit varies considerably with the variety, degree of maturity, preliminary treatment, temperature, humidity and volume of air, tray-load, degree of dryness desired, and other factors. It is therefore impossible to give a standard drying time for each fruit. The following times, however, observed in the University Farm dehydrater and other successful commercial dehydraters may be considered as normal. Unless otherwise noted, these times refer only to the air-blast tunnel dehydrater operated on the counter current system.

Using a finishing temperature of 165° F., apricots were dehydrated in from 9 to 15 hours, averaging 12 hours. At 160° F., unpeeled peaches required 20 to 30 hours, averaging 24 hours, while peeled peaches required only 14 hours. Unpeeled pears dried in 36 to 48 hours when finished at 150° F. Sliced pears required only 6 to 8 hours and peeled halves 16 to 18 hours at the same temperature. Drying time for French prunes varied from 18 to 30 hours, except in natural draft evaporators in which 30 to 36 hours was normal. The average drying time in air-blast dehydraters in 1920 was 24 hours for prunes, based on ample air flow and a finishing temperature of 165° F. At least 6 hours should be added to these times in the case of Imperial prunes. The maximum drying time for any variety of grapes at the University Farm was 30 hours. These grapes had been lye-dipped and were finished at 165° F. Most wine grapes required only 24 hours and Sultanina (Thompson seedless) grapes were dried in 15 hours. Sliced apples did not require over 8 hours to dry in an air-blast dehydrater at 160° F., while in a stack evaporator 18 hours were needed. By using a high initial temperature (200° F.) the time can be reduced to 2 hours. Using the parallel current system, starting at 210° F. and finishing at 170° F., dipped cherries were dried in 4 to 5 hours.

COMPARATIVE YIELDS AND QUALITIES OF SUN-DRIED AND DEHYDRATED FRUITS

Accurately controlled comparisons of sun-drying and dehydration of apricots, peaches, pears, and prunes were made at the University Farm. Uniform lots of several hundred pounds of each fruit were used. With the cut fruits, the two halves of each individual fruit were placed on separate trays, one lot of several trays being sun-dried in the customary way and the other lot dehydrated during regular operation of the dehydrater. Before drying, both lots were sulfured the usual time for sun-dried fruit. Prunes were uniformly mixed and, after dipping and rinsing, were divided equally between field and dehydrater trays. By such precautions, fruit of the same condition was used for the two methods of drying and any subsequent differences in the dried product were a direct result of the method of drying.

After drying the fruit was again carefully weighed and representative samples withdrawn which were later analyzed for moisture and sugar. The figures obtained are given in Table IV.

In the case of peaches and apricots, dehydration gave a slightly greater weight of dried fruit, but when considered on a uniform moisture content of 25 per cent, this greater yield was shown to be entirely due to the higher moisture content allowed to remain in the dehydrated product. In fact, the sun-dried lots show slightly greater yields of dry matter which is at least partly to be attributed to dust and sand accumulated during drying. With prunes, the sugar determinations reveal no significant differences between the two methods of drying. Various lots were dried so nearly to the same moisture content that the slight differences in yield noted are considered to be within the experimental error. No moisture or sugar determinations were made on the dried pears, but it was obvious that the lower yield of dehydrated pears was due principally to their lower moisture content, caused by over-drying. Similar results were obtained on grapes in 1919.

The dehydrated apricots were graded as "Growers Brand" by the California Prune and Apricot Growers, Inc., and brought 1½ cents per pound less than "Sunsweet Brand." This discrimination was made because the dehydrated fruit retained the color which the fruit

TABLE IV

COMPARATIVE YIELDS BY SUN-DRYING AND DEHYDRATION OF VARIOUS FRUITS

Fruits and method of drying	Drying ratio	Moisture in dry fruit, per cent	Pounds dry fruit per 100 pounds fresh		Per cent of sugar in dry fruit	
			As weighed from tray	On 25% water basis	As weighed from tray	On 25% water basis
Apricots						
In sun	5.1:1	15.6	19.7	22.1	50.1	47.5
In Univ. dehydrater	4.6:1	25.8	21.6	21.4	43.8	47.2
Apricots						
In sun	5.3:1	14.5	18.9	21.6	48.3	45.2
In stack evaporator	4.7:1	28.4	21.0	20.0	40.2	44.9
Peaches						
In sun	4.8:1	17.8	20.9	22.9	49.1	44.8
In Univ. dehydrater	4.5:1	23.7	22.1	22.5	47.9	47.0
Prunes						
In sun	1.5:1	15.7	68.0	76.2	....	....
In Univ. dehydrater	1.5:1	14.9	66.7	75.7	....	....
Prunes						
In sun	1.5:1	15.0	66.2	74.8	....	....
In Univ. dehydrater	1.5:1	14.4	67.1	76.3	....	....
Pears						
In sun	4.6:1	....	21.5	....	....	....
In Univ. dehydrater	5.0:1	....	20.1	....	....	....
Peaches						
In sun	4.5:1	17.8	22.5	24.6	49.1	44.9
In stack	4.5:1	17.3	22.5	24.8	48.3	43.9

had at the time of cutting. Green colored fresh fruit came from the dehydrater green in color, while similar fruit placed in the sun acquired a uniform golden yellow color, although still "green'" in flavor. The dehydrated fruit was opaque rather than translucent. When green apricots were avoided in picking, the thoroughly ripe fruit yielded a dehydrated product of a beautiful golden color, rivaling if not surpassing the sun-dried fruit. In quality, the dehydrated fruit was found much superior to the sun-dried. It absorbed water quickly and regained its full size during overnight soaking in water. It cooked more quickly than the sun-dried article and when used in sauces, pies, or puddings, very closely resembled fresh apricots prepared in the same way.

Profiting by the previous experience with apricots, only thoroughly ripe peaches were dehydrated, the product being accepted as first grade at the packing-house. The packer stated, however, that the dehydrated peaches were inferior in color and less "springy" than the sun-dried, which merely meant that the product was different from the customary sun-dried peaches. After refreshing in water, and cooking, the dehydrated peaches possessed a color and a flavor more closely resembling those of the fresh fruit than did the sun-dried. The peeled dehydrated peaches were especially good.

Dehydrated prunes are in general lighter in color than the sun-dried. This is particularly true of the flesh, which is invariably of a light amber color. Dehydrated prunes are usually cleaner and have a bright glossy appearance. When cooked, the flavor is excellent, resembling more closely that of the cooked fresh fruit. This may or may not be an advantage, depending on the consumer's preference for the usual sun-dried product.

Dehydrated unpeeled pears, even when sulfured 72 hours before drying, were not translucent like sun-dried pears but were chalky white. If the fruit is first partially dried in the sun and finished in a dehydrater, a translucent product is obtainable. Dehydrated pears, especially peeled and cored halves, are greatly superior in flavor to sun-dried pears, closely resembling fresh fruit after cooking.

Dehydrated wine grapes are unquestionably superior to the sun-dried for the making of beverages since they yield a juice of fresh color and flavor after being soaked in water and pressed. On the other hand, dehydrated Muscat grapes, even when dried without preliminary dipping or sulfuring, do not resemble the sun-dried raisins in flavor. In all instances, but especially when the grapes were dipped and sulfured, the dehydrated product retained a lighter color and a fresh Muscat flavor and not the well known raisin flavor resulting from sun-drying. The dehydrated Muscat can not be considered a direct competitior of "Sun-Maid" raisins, but is nevertheless an excellent product, which may in time create for itself a distinct market. A similar comparison may be made between dehydrated and sun-dried Sultanina (Thompson Seedless) grapes, although because of the lack of a distinctive flavor in these grapes, the differences were principally in appearance rather than in flavor. Dehydrated bleached Sultaninas were not translucent like the sun-dried, but otherwise were an excellent product.

Comparison of Sun-Drying and Stack-Drying: A comparison of sun-drying and stack-drying, using peaches, was made in the same way as between sun-drying and dehydration. One lot was spread in the sun for three days and the trays were then stacked for five days, the total drying time being eight days. The second lot was stacked immediately after sulfuring and at no time exposed to the direct rays of the sun. The drying time in this case was eleven days. The yields and the sugar contents of the two products as given at the bottom of Table IV are practically identical. The stack-dried fruit was

Fig. 1. Small air-blast tunnel dehydrater in Fruit Products Laboratory.

similar in color to the dehydrated peaches in that unripe fruit remained green in color after drying and ripe fruit was paler yellow in color than when sun-dried. The stack-dried peaches were cleaner in appearance and slightly better in flavor than the sun-dried.

Sulfurous-Acid Content of Sun-Dried and Dehydrated Fruits: Samples of pears, apricots, and seedless raisins which had been

TABLE V

SULFUR DIOXIDE IN SUN-DRIED AND DEHYDRATED FRUITS

Fruits and method of drying	Hours sulfured	Sulfur dioxide, parts per million	Remarks
Pears			
University dehydrater..........	1	70	
University dehydrater..........	2	191	
University dehydrater..........	4	645	
University dehydrater..........	24	632	From same lot of pears
Sun	2	270	
Sun	4	536	
Sun and shade	24+	765	Sample from trays— Lake County
University dehydrater..........	3	344	Peeled halves
University dehydrater..........	24+	736	Average for season
Apricots			
University dehydrater..........	1	236	Comparative lots
Sun	1	706	
University dehydrater..........	3	1329	Comparative lots
Sun	3	1068	
Stack evaporator..................	3	937	Average sample
University dehydrater..........	3	678	Comparative lots
Sun	3	702	
Seedless grapes (Sultanina)			
University dehydrater..........	½	403	
University dehydrater..........	2	910	
University dehydrater..........	4	678	Exposed to sun 3 hours
Stack evaporator..................	4	408	
Stack evaporator..................	2	1188	Exposed to sun 3 hours

1000 parts per million equals 0.1 per cent.

sulfured various lengths of time and dried in different ways were analyzed for sulfur dioxide, with the results shown in Table V. The samples had not been subjected to the resulfuring commonly given before packing and therefore contain less sulfur dioxide than is normally found in commercial samples. It is evident that the amount of sulfur dioxide absorbed by the fruit and retained after drying increases with the time of exposure to sulfur fumes. Since dehydrated fruits require only a very short sulfuring, in general not over one hour, they contain much less sulfur dioxide than similar fruit sulfured many hours preliminary to sun-drying. Dehydrated fruits come from the dehydrater clean and sterile and, if properly stored and packed, need not be resulfured, thereby eliminating any objection on the part of the consumer because of "sulfurous" fruit.

STEMMING

The stemming of dehydrated grapes gave considerable trouble .during the past season largely because of insufficient drying, sweating of dehydrated grapes in bins before stemming, or improper adjustment of stemming machines. Unless dehydrated grapes were stemmed soon after drying, the grapes and stems stuck to the stemmer and formed masses of the unstemmed grapes. Where grapes were allowed to stand or sweat after removal from the dehydrater, the dry brittle stems reabsorbed water from the grapes or the air and became flexible, preventing them from breaking from the berries readily. The absorption of moisture by the stems also caused them to increase in specific gravity, increasing the difficulty of fanning out the stems. A blast strong enough to remove the stems caused loss of small dried grapes in the stemmer waste. Insufficiently dried grapes presented the same difficulties.

The dried grapes did not stem satisfactorily when they contained more than 15 per cent of moisture. If the grapes are sticky from heavy steaming or dipping, they should contain only 12 per cent or less for satisfactory stemming. Grapes dried without dipping were stemmed at a higher moisture content than steamed or dipped grapes. At the University Farm in 1920, the grapes were dried to from 13 to 15 per cent moisture and stemmed as soon as removed from the dehydrater. With careful adjustment of the stemmer, excellent results were obtained.

Cherries may be stemmed satisfactorily by machinery before drying but the stemming is best done after drying. Ordinary raisin stemmers can probably be adjusted for this purpose. On a small scale, the stems can be quickly removed by rubbing the dried cherries on a screen tray of ⅜ to ½ inch mesh. The brittle stems break off and drop through the screen.

PROCESSING

Laboratory experiments and the experience of several commercial plants demonstrated that steaming of stemmed grapes affords a simple and effective means of returning to the dried product the moisture ' necessary to replace that removed to make stemming possible. This represents the difference between about 14 and 22 per cent, or a total of 8 per cent.

A very satisfactory system of processing dried grapes developed in one plant, consisted in scraping the trays into a hopper from which a conveyor carried the grapes to the stemmer. The stemmed grapes discharged on to a second conveyor, which carried them through a long narrow box filled with an abundance of live steam. The hot processed grapes discharged directly into the packing box. The grapes absorbed water at the rate of 3 to 4 per cent per minute, the time of processing being regulated by the speed of the conveyor. The steamed grapes were bright and clean in appearance. Grapes processed in hot water lost much color and sugar and were duller in color. In some plants, the desired amount of water was added to the piles of stemmed raisins which were then thoroughly mixed by shoveling in order to equalize the moisture. This method is neither cheap nor sanitary and does not sterilize insect eggs.

The processing and packing of prunes gave trouble in several packing houses in 1920. When deliveries of dehydrated prunes containing over 20 per cent of moisture were mixed with sun-dried prunes of 16 per cent or less moisture, and the resulting mixture processed in hot water in the usual way, the tender and moister dehydrated prunes absorbed so much water that they not only tended to disintegrate but were liable to mould after packing. If prunes are not over-dipped nor dried at such a high temperature as to cause cracking, and finally are dried to the same moisture content as sun-dried prunes, they may be readily processed and packed in the same manner now used for sun-dried prunes. It is always best, however, to keep dehydrated prunes separate in order that the time of processing may be adjusted to their moisture content. Since prunes as well as all dehydrated fruits come from the dehydrater clean and sterile, it should not be necessary to over-dry them and then return part of the moisture by dipping. Where it is necessary to store the fruit for some time in large bins for blending or other purposes, steam processing is the most satisfactory way of sterilizing the product.

MOISTURE CONTENT

The United States Department of Agriculture has placed the legal limit for moisture in dried apples at 24 per cent. It is likely that similar standards will in time be adopted for all dried fruits. When this is done, accurate control of moisture in the finished product will become a necessity. But it is always to the interest of the producer to market his product with the maximum amount of moisture which will permit it to keep indefinitely. In order to have a careful check on the moisture content, it is highly desirable for every plant to make frequent moisture determinations on representative samples. In order to obtain dependable results, it is of primary importance to sample fairly large quantities after thorough mixing. About one pound of pitted fruit is then taken and ground through a food chopper.

The official method of determining moisture in dried fruits consists in drying a 10 gram sample for exactly 12 hours in a vacuum oven at 158° F. and at a vacuum of 29 inches mercury. This method necessitates the use of equipment costing several hundred dollars and is time-consuming. A modification of this method, used in the Fruit Products Laboratory, consists in employing a temperature of 200° F. and a vacuum of 29 inches mercury for exactly two hours. It has been shown that this more rapid method gives results sufficiently close to the official method for commercial purposes.

A simpler but less reliable and less rapid method consists in drying a 10 gram sample for a specified time in a steam or hot water jacketed oven at 212° F. The times usually adopted are 3½ hours for apricots, 4½ hours for peaches, 4 hours for apples, 5 hours for pears, 4 hours for grapes, and 3 hours for prunes. The loss in weight in each instance multiplied by ten represents the percentage of moisture.

Experiments in progress since 1919 show that dehydrated grapes containing not more than 23 per cent of moisture will keep indefinitely. Samples containing 23 to 30 per cent of moisture sooner or later become mouldy, while those above 30 per cent soon ferment unless heavily sulfured to prevent spoiling.

Prunes containing more than 25 per cent of moisture in most instances become mouldy.

Moisture standards for dried peaches, apricots, and pears are more difficult to determine because of the complication caused by the preservative effect of varying concentrations of sulfurous acid in these products.

COST OF DEHYDRATION

The costs of dehydration, both operating costs and fixed charges, are discussed in a report of this Station entitled, "Some Factors Affecting Dehydrater Efficiency." The operating costs for the dehydration of apricots, peaches, pears, and grapes in the University Farm dehydrater are given in Table VI. The total costs given in this table should not be taken as typical of commercial operation because

TABLE VI

APPROXIMATE OPERATING COST OF DEHYDRATING VARIOUS FRUITS IN THE UNIVERSITY FARM DEHYDRATER

Item	Apricots		Peaches		Pears		Grapes	
	Per green ton	Per dry ton	Per green ton	Per dry ton	Per green ton	Per dry ton	Per green ton	Per dry ton
Cutting, 20c per box	$8.00	$46.40	$7.51	$35.82	$6.78	$30.51	....	....
Labor, tray men and operator, 50c per hour	3.66	21.23	3.40	16.22	4.26	19.17	$4.16	$14.56
Fuel, stove oil, 8c per gallon for drying and dipping	1.36	7.89	1.99	9.49	3.48	15.66	3.62	12.67
Electricity, power and light, 3.7c per k.w. hour	.30	1.74	.40	1.91	.50	2.25	.45	1.50
Sulfur, 3.5c per lb.	.15	.87	.20	.96	.42	1.89	.05	.18
Lye, 7c per lb.	......	....	....	....	....	....	.28	.98
Total operating cost	$13.47	$78.13	$13.50	$64.40	$15.44	$69.48	$8.56	$29.89

considerable extra expense, principally for labor and fuel, was incurred in the conduct of experiments. On the other hand, the salary of a superintendent is not included, his duties having been performed by the writers. The cost of dehydration in commercial operations should not exceed that of sun-drying, since the extra cost of fuel and power may be largely offset by the decreased cost of labor in handling trays.

Owing to the fact that the transformers and motor used at the University Farm Dehydrater were not large enough to operate the fan at the desired speed and also because of the undesirable position of the fan discharge, the air flow was inadequate for most economical operation. These defects can be readily remedied. The drying time was considerably longer than if ample air flow had been available. This, together with the fact that the dehydrater was not always operated at full capacity, made certain costs, such as fuel, power, and operator's wages, greater than would otherwise be necessary.

In the case of grapes, about one-fourth of the fuel consumed was used for dipping and about 10 per cent of the power cost was utilized in operation of the stemmer. In two commercial plants, the total operating costs for the dehydration of grapes were $12.83 and $8.80 per green ton, respectively.

The cost of dehydration of prunes as obtained in four commercial plants is given in Table VII. The three air-blast dehydraters referred to are all of fairly satisfactory design, the operating costs being approximately equal. The greater cost of fuel in the stack evaporator is caused by lack of air recirculation. Recirculation of air is an essential factor in fuel economy. The greater labor cost in the stack evaporator is necessitated by individual handling of trays as compared to the truck load movement of trays in tunnel dehydraters.

The cost of dehydrating apples in one large plant in 1920 was given as $115 per dry ton, which included $10 for box shook, $5 for fuel, and $100 for labor. Since the charge for custom drying was $125 per dry ton, this would leave only $10 per dry ton for fixed charges and profit. In another plant, the labor cost was shown to be $90, the fuel $8.40, and the power $3.90 per dry ton.

TABLE VII

TYPICAL OPERATING COSTS IN PRUNE DEHYDRATERS

Type of dehydrater	Cost per green ton			
	Labor	Fuel	Power	Total
University Farm type	$5.88	$1.27	$ .90	$8.05
Air-blast tunnel	5.30	2.10	1.00	8.40
Air-blast tunnel	6.00	1.65	1.40	9.05
Stack type, natural draft	12.53	3.29	.10	15.92

MISCELLANEOUS FRUITS

In addition to the investigations already reported, less extensive experiments have been made in the dehydration of figs, berries, olives, persimmons, and citrus fruits.

Figs: In 1919, about seventy-five pounds of Mission figs were dried in the sun at the University Farm and two lots of similar fruit were dehydrated. Of the latter, one lot was dipped in dilute, boiling lye solution and rinsed in water, while the other was untreated. They were dehydrated at not above 150° F. Both of the dehydrated lots were slightly over-dried, as they were placed on a car with grapes, which require a longer drying period. The drying time was less than fifteen hours, the dipped fruit drying more rapidly than the undipped.

The surface of the dehydrated fruit was glossy after drying, particularly that which had been lye dipped. Both dehydrated lots were satisfactory in every respect and superior in flavor and cooking quality to the sun-dried product.

"Calimyrna" figs from Merced were received at the University Farm dehydrater in 1920. The fruit was well ripened but some of it had begun to sour in transit. It was divided into three lots. One was dehydrated untreated on screen trays; another, dehydrated after sulfuring for six hours on slat trays; and the figs of the third lot were slit down one side, as in the packing of dried figs in brick form, and spread apart upon trays. Nine hours at 165° F. was required to dry the whole fruit. The slit fruit dried much more rapidly. No noticeable injury to color or flavor occurred in drying at 165° F. The slit fruit presented a glossy surface and attractive appearance. The sulfured figs were slightly lighter in color but were not quite so attractive in flavor as the unsulfured. The "sour" or fermented flavor, which was noticeable in a great deal of the fresh fruit, completely disappeared during dehydration, a fact which should interest those who grow white figs in sections where souring and splitting occur. These preliminary experiments indicate the possibility of fig dehydration, but further investigation is needed to establish proper procedures, costs, etc.

· *Strawberries:* Several of the important commercial varieties of strawberries were dehydrated experimentally. The fruit was shipped direct from the grower to the dehydrater within less than 24 hours after picking.

At temperatures above 130° F., the fresh fruit "leaked" badly, losing a great deal of its juice. The best results were obtained by starting drying at 110° F. and progressively increasing the temperature to 160° F. Twenty-six to twenty-eight hours' drying time was required under these conditions. The finished product was of unattractive appearance but of excellent flavor. The dehydrated berries were very satisfactory for use in preparing preserves, jams and pies. Sulfuring for one half hour before dehydration improved the color. Halved berries dried more rapidly and were more attractive in appearance than the whole fruit, but the cost of such a method of preparation would be excessive.

Loganberries: Firm, ripe, freshly picked loganberries yielded a dehydrated product of excellent flavor and color, with the individual berries equal in size to the original fresh fruit. Over-ripe and bruised berries lost considerable juice by dripping and tended to form "slabs." The parallel current system was used successfully. The drying was started at 200° F. and 6 per cent relative humidity, and was completed at 160° F. and 30 per cent relative humidity. Seven to eight hours' drying time was required with the above temperature range and an air velocity of 975 feet per minute.

Raspberries: Raspberries were dehydrated without preliminary treatment. A dehydrated product of excellent color and flavor was obtained by starting drying at 189° F. and 10 per cent relative humidity and finishing at 160° F. Using air at a velocity of 975 feet per minute, drying was completed in 4½ hours.

Olives: Pickled ripe olives, dehydrated at 350° F. or above, remained plump and equal in size to the original fruit. The flavor of the dehydrated product was pleasing, although, when stored in the open air, the fruit became rancid. Storage in vacuum-sealed containers would probably overcome this difficulty.

When dried at temperatures of 160° F. to 250° F., the fruit was badly shriveled, although superior in flavor to that dehydrated at 350° F.

Shredded ripe olives were dried in 3 hours at 210° F. to 220° F. The product was of rich flavor and suitable for cooking in macaroni, spaghetti, meat pies, and many other dishes. The drying ratio of the shredded olive flesh was 3:1. It is possible that small sizes of olives might be utilized in this way.

Persimmons: Persimmons are dried in large quantities in Japan and China by placing the peeled, ripe fruit on strings in the shade. The finished product is brown, soft, sticky, and very sweet. It is free from the "puckery taste" of unripe persimmons.

Attempts to dehydrate peeled, whole, ripe fruit proved that an excessively long drying period (more than 48 hours at 150° F. to 165° F.) was necessary. Excellent results were obtained by peeling and slicing the firm, ripe fruit and drying it without further treatment. Even very astringent fruit became sweet and free from "pucker" when dried in this manner. Sulfuring the sliced fruit, even for so short a period as fifteen minutes, gave an intensely astringent, dried product and did not materially improve the color.

The dehydrated fruit refreshed well on soaking in water. It also made a pleasing confection when eaten in the dry state. The yield was approximately one pound of dry to three pounds of fresh fruit.

Bananas: In the tropics, bananas are usually dried in the sun after peeling. Such dried fruit is dark brown and of unattractive appearance. It is marketed under the name of "banana figs." A dried product of higher quality is produced commercially by artificial heat, although the industry is still small. Large quantities of bananas go to waste in banana-exporting countries. Dehydration would afford a simple means of preventing this waste by putting the fruit in a form suitable for export to other countries. Experiments in the Fruit Products Laboratory demonstrated that a dried product of attractive appearance and pleasing flavor could be made from bananas in the

Fig. 2.—Upper left: Coöperative dehydrater built by Farm Bureau at Placerville. Lower left: Building a University Farm dehydrater at Los Gatos. Right: Unloading trays at University Farm dehydrater, Davis.

following manner. The ripe fruit was peeled and sliced longitudinally in halves or in strips about a quarter of an inch in thickness. It was then spread on trays, sulfured for twenty to thirty minutes, and dehydrated. A temperature of 200° F. was used while the fruit still contained a large amount of water, but 165° F. should not be exceeded during the last stages of drying. Twenty per cent moisture in the finished product gave a very desirable texture. The drying ratio of the peeled fruit was approximately 3:1; of the unpeeled fruit, 4.5:1.

The fruit in the dry state was satisfactory for confection or dessert purposes or, after soaking overnight in water or milk, for cakes, puddings or pies.

Citrus Fruits: Oranges and lemons have been dried upon a commercial scale by artificial heat without other treatment than slicing and placing on trays. The fruit has been dried "bone dry" and ground to a powder and used in bakeries and restaurants for pastry purposes.

Orange and lemon peels are also dried, either in the sun or by artificial heat, for the preparation of extracts and flavors. For this purpose only the outer yellow portion of the peel is desired. The market is limited.

Our experiments demonstrate that a good lemonade may be made from dried, sliced, unpeeled lemons. A short sulfuring before drying gives a lighter colored product. Dried citrus fruit juices in powdered form have been produced in spray driers, such as are used for drying milk.

TABLE VIII

RECOMMENDED METHODS FOR DEHYDRATION OF VARIOUS FRUITS

Variety of fruit	Pounds per sq. ft. on trays	Hours sulfured	Maximum temperature at end of drying period	Desirable humidity in tunnel dehydrater at end of drying period	Drying time by counter current method, hours	Remarks
Apples	2	½	165° F.	5–10%	8	Peeled and sliced or cubed
Apricots	2	1	160° F.	10%	12	Halves unpeeled
Apricots	2	½	160° F.	10%	8	Sliced
Bananas	1–2	½	165° F.	5–10%	12–18	Peeled, cut in half lengthwise
Cherries						
Black Tartarian	2–3	0	170° F.	10–25%	8–12	Lye dipped
Royal Anne	2–3	¼	170° F.	10–25%	8–12	Lye dipped
Figs	2–3	1	160° F.	5%	10	One side cut and figs spread open
Grapes						
Muscat	3½–4	0	160° F.	5%	24	Lye dipped
Seedless	3½–4	1	160° F.	5%	16	Lye dipped
Wine	3½–4	1	160° F.	5%	20	Lye dipped
Loganberries	1½–2	0	160° F.	10–25%	10–15	Untreated
Peaches	3	1	150° F.	10–20%	24	Not peeled
Peaches	3	1	150° F.	10–20%	16	Lye peeled
Pears	3	24	145° F.	20%	48	Halves unpeeled
Pears	2	½	150° F.	10–20%	6	Peeled and sliced
Pears	2	1	150° F.	10%	16	Peeled and cored
Prunes						
French	2½–4	0	165° F.	5–10%	24	Lye dipped
Imperial	3–4	0	165° F.	10–20%	30–36	Lightly dipped
Raspberries	1½–2	0	170° F.	10–25%	8–12	Untreated
Strawberries	1½–2	½	160° F.	10–25%	24	Stemmed

SUMMARY

The results reported in this Bulletin are summarized in Table VIII, where are listed in brief form the tested methods of preparation and conditions of dehydration recommended for various fruits. These recommendations apply to the air-blast tunnel type of dehydrater, which so far has proved the most satisfactory type for general fruit dehydration.

Further investigations in the dehydration of fruits are under way and many operators of dehydraters are also experimenting on various phases of dehydration. It is fully expected therefore that many of the present practices of dehydration may be greatly modified during the next few years. Therefore, it may be necessary to revise the recommendations given in Table VIII as our knowledge of the dehydration of fruit increases.

ACKNOWLEDGMENTS

The investigations reported in this bulletin were made possible by funds from the appropriation for Deciduous Fruit Investigations made by the state legislature of 1919.

The writers are indebted to the many manufacturers, owners, and operators of dehydraters whose generous coöperation made possible the securing of much valuable data. Grateful appreciation is extended to the California Pear Growers' Association; G. H. Hecke of Woodland; E. P. Phillips of Winters; Boyce and Boyce Ranch, Mr. Wurman, Manager, of Winters, and F. W. Yokum of Merced for much of the fruit used in the experiments at the University Farm. Thanks are also due to the Pacific Wann Evaporator Co., and the Cutler Dry Kiln Co., for the use of equipment installed at the University Farm. The valuable coöperation of G. B. Ridley and G. R. Kline, of the Heinemann-Pearson Co., of San Francisco, is gratefully acknowledged.

The writers also express their appreciation to Professor F. T. Bioletti for helpful revision of the manuscript.

www.ingramcontent.com/pod-product-compliance
Lightning Source LLC
Chambersburg PA
CBHW021917040426
42447CB00007B/901